GELATIN & PUDDING SHOT RECIPES

Mom Never Made It Like THIS!

Volume 3

By: Lisa Doherty

GELATIN & PUDDING SHOT RECIPES

Mom Never Made It Like THIS!

Volume 3

Lisa Doherty

Layout & cover work: Lisa Doherty
Printing & publication: Lulu.com
Website: stores.lulu.com/leezil

ISBN-13: 978-0-557-00168-2

Table of Contents

Foreword

This book goes out to all of you pudding lovers out there - you know who you are! There was a very good response to the pudding shots I included in the last book, so I decided to expand on them even more in this one! This book contains some candy and dessert recipes of the pudding variety. While they may not taste *exactly* like the original, it is pretty darn close!!

For the gelatin, we have some classic drinks, tasty treats and a few creations of my own. There are a lot of fun recipes in here, like Dew Me on the Beach and Nuclear Kamikaze. Some of the mild ones have a nice fruity flavor, such as Starburst and Mango Peach Mélange. But ... if strong is what you are looking for, try a Home Wrecker or Strawberry Long Island Iced Tea!

Unlike gelatin, making pudding is not an exact science. Upon perfecting the pudding recipes, I found that it may not always weigh what it says on the box. This could affect the consistency of your shot, making it too thick or too thin. Unless you weigh each pouch of pudding and adjust the amount of half and half according, there is no way of getting around this. All I can suggest is to keep experimenting!

Thank you to all of my oh-so-willing taste testers! Your wonderful feedback helped me to create this masterpiece before you.

Enjoy!

Gelatin Shot Directions

Gelatin Directions #1

Step 1	Bring water to a boil
Step 2	Measure out 1 cup of water into a large container with a pouring spout
Step 3	Add gelatin and stir for 2 minutes until dissolved
Step 4	Measure out remainder of the ingredients
Step 5	Pour ingredients into gelatin and stir well
Step 6	Pour gelatin into individual soufflé cups and arrange on a large tray
Step 7	Place lids on shots
Step 8	Place tray in refrigerator for shots to solidify, about 4 hours

Gelatin Directions #2

Follow Gelatin Directions #1, except in Step 1, instead of bringing water to a boil, boil soda in a microwave safe dish for 2 to 3 minutes (every microwave is different), and measure out 1 cup. Continue with Step 3.

Tip: All gelatin recipes use the 3 ounce size box.

Cape Cod Cooler

1c. Boiling Water
1 box Cranberry Gelatin
1/2c. Sloe Gin
1/4c. Gin
1/8c. Amaretto
1/8c. Water
Dash of Lime Juice

Tip: Whipped cream is yummy on top of any shot!

Caribbean Queen

1c. Boiling Water
1 box Lemon Gelatin
1/4c. Coconut Rum
1/4c. Watermelon Schnapps
1/8c. Triple Sec
3/8c. Orange Juice

Cherry Sweet Tart

1c. Boiling Water
1 box Cherry Gelatin
1/4c. Southern Comfort®
1/4c. Amaretto
1/2c. Sweet and Sour Mix
1T. Grenadine

Note: To cut down on the tartness, only use 1/4c. sweet & sour mix and 1/4c. water

Chocolate Covered Strawberry

1c. Boiling Water
1 box Strawberry Gelatin
1/3c. Strawberry Schnapps
1/3c. Dark Crème de Cacao
1/3c. Strawberry Soda

Dew Me on the Beach

1c. Boiling Water
1 box Pineapple Gelatin
1/2c. Coconut Rum
1/2c. Mountain Dew Soda

Georgian Sunrise

1c. Boiling Water
1 box Peach Gelatin
3/8c. Tequila
1/4c. Strawberry Schnapps
1/8c. Peach Schnapps
1/4c. Sweet & Sour Mix

Grape Strawberry Daiquiri

1c. Boiling Water
1 box Grape Gelatin
1/4c. Light Rum
1/2c. Strawberry Schnapps
1/4c. Strawberry Soda

Note: Try using strawberry gelatin, grape schnapps and grape soda for a different flavor.

Hawaiian Humdinger

1c. Boiling Water
1 box Pineapple Gelatin
1/2c. Gin
1/8c. Triple Sec
3/8c. Water

Home Wrecker

1c. Boiling Water
1 box Cranberry Gelatin
1/4c. Tequila
1/4c. Melon Liqueur
1/8c. Jagermeister®
3/8c. Water

Tip: Do not use straight alcohol, or the gelatin shots will not completely set.

Incredible Hulk

1c. Boiling Water
1 box Melon Fusion Gelatin
1/4c. Vodka
1/4c. Melon Liqueur
1/8c. Triple Sec
3/8c. Water
Splash of Sweet & Sour Mix

Jamaican Me Crazy

1c. Boiling Water
1 box Tropical Fusion Gelatin
1/4c. Light Rum
1/4c. Coconut Rum
1/8c. Banana Liqueur
3/8c. Water

Note: If Tropical Fusion is not available, try using Mixed Fruit gelatin instead.

Jolly Rancher

1c. Boiling Water
1 box Cranberry Gelatin
1/2c. Vodka
1/4c. Melon Liqueur
1/4c. Water

Knoxville Lemonade

1c. Boiling Water
1 box Lemon Gelatin
1/4c. Vodka
1/4c. Peach Schnapps
1/2c. Ginger Ale

Mango Peach Mélange

1c. Boiling Water
1 box Peach Gelatin
1/2c. Mango Rum
1/4c. Peach Schnapps
1/4c. Water

Mega Berry Blast

1c. Boiling Water
1 box Berry Fusion Gelatin
1/8c. Vodka
1/8c. Blue Curacao
1/8c. Vanilla Liqueur
1/8c. Strawberry Schnapps
1/8c. Raspberry Schnapps
1/8c. Grenadine
1/4c. Water

Note: Any berry flavor will work if Berry Fusion is not available.

Mimosa

1c. Boiling Water
1 box Orange Gelatin
2/3c. Champagne
1/3c. Orange Juice

Note: The shots will look a little cloudy

Nuclear Kamikaze

1c. Boiling Water
1 box Lime Gelatin
3/8c. Vodka
1/4c. Melon Liqueur
1/8c. Triple Sec
1/4c. Water

Tip: Make shots with a friend! While one person is dissolving the gelatin, have the other measuring out the cold ingredients. Afterwards, while one person is pouring, the other can put lids on. You'd be surprised how fast the process goes!

Orange Crush

1c. Boiling Water
1 box Orange Gelatin
3/8c. Vodka
3/8c. Triple Sec
1/4c. Water

Raspberry Lemonade Martini

1c. Boiling Water
1 box Raspberry Gelatin
1/4c. Citrus Vodka
1/4c. Raspberry Liqueur
1/2c. Lemonade

Note: For a more lemony taste, boil lemonade instead of water, and follow Gelatin Directions #2

Red Square Martini

1c. Boiling Water
1 box Cherry Gelatin
1/4c. Citrus Vodka
1/8c. Sour Apple Schnapps
1/8c. Triple Sec
1/8c. Lemon Jc.
3/8c. Water
1T. Grenadine

Sea Breeze

1c. Boiling Water
1 box Cranberry Gelatin
1/2c. Vodka
1/2c. Grapefruit Juice

Tip: Make sure you have all of the ingredients before you make the gelatin.

Spiced Cherry

1c. Boiling Dr Pepper Soda
1 box Cherry Gelatin
2/3c. Spiced Rum
1/3c. Dr Pepper Soda

Note: Follow Gelatin Directions #2 for this recipe

Starburst

1c. Boiling Water
1 box Lemon Gelatin
3/8c. Strawberry Schnapps
3/8c. Watermelon Schnapps
1/4c. Water

Strawberry Long Island Iced Tea

1c. Boiling Strawberry Soda
1 box Strawberry Gelatin
1/8c. Gin
1/8c. Light Rum
1/8c. Vodka
1/8c. Tequila
1/8c. Triple Sec
1/4c. plus 1T. Strawberry Soda
1 T. Lemon Juice

Note: Follow Gelatin Directions #2 for this recipe

Turquoise Treasure

1c. Boiling Water
1 box Berry Blue Gelatin
3/8c. Spiced Rum
1/4c. Blue Curacao
1/8c. Vanilla Liqueur
1/4c. Water

Tip: As a cost cutting measure, go to a liquor store to purchase one ounce bottles of unusual liquors that you wouldn't use very often.

Pudding Shot Directions

<u>Pudding Directions</u>

Step 1 Measure out half and half into a large container with a pouring spout

Step 2 Measure alcohol and add to half and half

Step 3 Add pudding mix

Step 4 Whisk for 2 minutes

Step 5 Pour pudding into individual soufflé cups and arrange on a large tray

Step 6 Place lids on shots

Step 7 Place tray in refrigerator for shots to thicken, about 2 hours

Tip: All recipes use the 3 ounce size box of instant pudding.

Banana Cream Pie

1- 1/2c. Half and Half
1 box Banana Instant Pudding
1/8c. Vodka
1/8c. Crème de Cacao
1T. Banana Liqueur

Note: I only listed Crème de Cacao in the Index, I didn't specify light or dark. There isn't much difference in taste, so if you only have one or another, it can be easily substituted.

Banana Split

1- 1/8c. Half and Half
1 box Vanilla Instant Pudding
1/8c. Coconut Rum
1/8c. Vanilla Vodka
1/8c. Strawberry Tequila Cream Liqueur
1/8c. Banana Liqueur
1/8c. Crème de Cacao

Blueberries & Cream

1- 3/8c. Half and Half
1 box Vanilla Instant Pudding
1/8c. Blueberry Vodka
1/8c. Irish Cream Liqueur
1/8c. Vanilla Liqueur

Butternut Rum Lifesaver

Note: Add the pineapple juice last before you mix. The mixture may start to curdle a little, but mix right away and it will blend nicely.

1- 1/4c. Half and Half
1 box Vanilla Instant Pudding
1/8c. Coconut Rum
1/8c. Irish Cream Liqueur
1/8c. Butterscotch Schnapps
1/8c. Pineapple Juice

Butterscotch Shooter

1- 1/4c. Half and Half
1 box Butterscotch Instant Pudding
1/4c. Butterscotch Schnapps
1/4c. Crème de Cacao

Tip: When pouring the pudding into the individual cups, a spoon & spatula will be handy to get all of the pudding out of the container.

Caramel Sundae

1- 1/4c. Half and Half
1 box Vanilla Instant Pudding
1/8c. Irish Cream Liqueur
1/8c. Hazelnut Liqueur
1/8c. Vodka
1/8c. Butterscotch Schnapps

Chocolate Cake

1- 1/8c. Half and Half
1 box Chocolate Instant Pudding
1/4c. Vanilla Vodka
1/8c. Coconut Rum
1/8c. Hazelnut Liqueur
1/8c. Crème de Cacao

Coconut Cream Pie

1- 1/8c. Half and Half
1 box Vanilla Instant Pudding
1/4c. Coconut Rum
1/4c. Vanilla Liqueur

Dirty Girl Scout

1- 1/4c. Half and Half
1 box Chocolate Instant Pudding
1/8c. Irish Cream Liqueur
1/8c. Coffee Liqueur
1/8c. Vodka
1 T. White Crème de Menthe

Tip: When purchasing the pudding mixes, make sure it is INSTANT pudding, not COOK & SERVE.

Gingerbread Man

1- 3/8c. Half and Half
1 box Vanilla Instant Pudding
1/8c. Coffee Liqueur
1/8c. Irish Cream Liqueur
1/8c. Cinnamon Schnapps

Irish Spirit

1- 1/4c. Half and Half
1 box Vanilla Instant Pudding
1/2c. Irish Cream Liqueur

Kryptonite

1- 3/8c. Half and Half
1 box Vanilla Instant Pudding
1/8c. Amaretto
1/8c. Irish Cream Liqueur
1/8c. Blue Curacao

Note: This shot tastes like Superman ice cream, but I changed the name to Kryptonite because once everything was mixed, it transformed into this lovely green color.

M&M

1- 1/4c. Half and Half
1 box Chocolate Instant Pudding
1/4c. Hazelnut Liqueur
1/4c. Crème de Cacao

Milky Way

1- 3/8c. Half and Half
1 box White Chocolate Instant Pudding
1/8c. Vanilla Vodka
1/8c. Irish Cream Liqueur
1/8c. Crème de Cacao
1 tsp. Butterscotch Schnapps

Mocha Mayhem

1- 1/8c. Half and Half
1 box Chocolate Instant Pudding
1/4c. Coffee Liqueur
1/4c. Crème de Cacao

Tip: You can use an electric mixer on low speed instead of a whip.

Moon Pie

1- 1/2c. Half and Half
1 box Chocolate Instant Pudding
1/8c. Coffee Liqueur
1/8c. Irish Cream Liqueur
1T. Banana Liqueur

Pink Rose

1- 1/4c. Half and Half
1 box Vanilla Instant Pudding
1/2c. Strawberry Tequila Cream Liqueur

Pumpkin Pie

1- 1/2c. Half and Half
1 box Butterscotch Instant Pudding
1/8c. Coffee Liqueur
1/8c. Irish Cream Liqueur
1/8c. Cinnamon Schnapps
2 Dashes Pumpkin Pie Spice

Note: There is a Pumpkin Spice pudding that is offered seasonally. If you can find it, try using it in this recipe!

Raspberry Rhapsody

1- 1/8c. Half and Half
1 box Chocolate Instant Pudding
1/4c. Raspberry Liqueur
1/4c. Crème de Cacao

Tip: If you don't have Raspberry Liqueur, Raspberry Schnapps can be substituted.

Snickers

1- 1/4c. Half and Half
1 box Chocolate Instant Pudding
1/4c. Dark Crème de Cacao
1/8c. Hazelnut Liqueur
1/8c. Irish Cream Liqueur

Spice Cake

1- 3/8c. Half and Half
1 box Vanilla Instant Pudding
1/8c. Amaretto
1/8c. Cinnamon Schnapps
1/8c. Irish Cream Liqueur

Strawberry Blonde

1- 1/8c. Half and Half
1 box Vanilla Instant Pudding
1/8c. Crème de Cacao
1/8c. Strawberry Tequila Cream Liqueur
1/4c. Irish Cream Liqueur

Tip: Try mixing Strawberry Quik with your half and half for even more strawberry flavor!

Three Musketeers

1- 3/8c. Half and Half
1 box Vanilla Instant Pudding
1/8c. Crème de Cacao
1/8c. Coffee Liqueur
1/8c. Irish Cream Liqueur

Tip: For a lighter, fluffier texture, use whipping cream instead of half and half.

Tootsie Roll

1- 3/8c. Half and Half
1 box Chocolate Instant Pudding
1/8c. Dark Crème de Cacao
1/8c. Hazelnut Liqueur
1/8c. Coffee Liqueur

Vanilla Quaalude

1- 1/4c. Half and Half
1 box Vanilla Instant Pudding
1/4c. Light Crème de Cacao
1/8c. Hazelnut Liqueur
1/8c. Vanilla Vodka

Tip: Labeling shots with small color coded stickers helps to identify them better, especially if you have different flavors that are the same color.

Index 1

This Index is arranged by Gelatin and Pudding Types.

Gelatin

Pudding

Vanilla (cont.)

White Chocolate

Index 2

This Index is arranged by Alcohol Type.

Index 2 (cont.)

Index 2 (cont.)

www.ingramcontent.com/pod-product-compliance
Ingram Content Group UK Ltd.
Pitfield, Milton Keynes, MK11 3LW, UK
UKHW041834200726
13854UKWH00003BA/1128